Social Progress and Sustainability

Shelter • Safety • Literacy • Health • Freedom • Environment

South America

Foreword by **Michael Green,**
Executive Director, Social Progress Imperative

By **Judy Boyd**

Social Progress and Sustainability

The Series:

Africa: Northern and Eastern

Africa: Middle, Western, and Southern

East Asia and the Pacific

Europe

Eurasia

Near East

South and Central Asia

North America

Central America and the Caribbean

South America

Social Progress and Sustainability

Shelter • Safety • Literacy • Health • Freedom • Environment

South America

Judy Boyd

Foreword by
Michael Green
Executive Director, Social Progress Imperative

MASON CREST

Mason Crest
450 Parkway Drive, Suite D
Broomall, PA 19008
www.masoncrest.com

Printed and bound in the United States of America

First printing
9 8 7 6 5 4 3 2 1

Series ISBN: 978-1-4222-3490-7
Hardcover ISBN: 978-1-4222-3499-0
ebook ISBN: 978-1-4222-8394-3

Library of Congress Cataloging-in-Publication Data

Names: Boyd, Judy, 1950– author.
Title: South America/Judy Boyd; foreword by Michael Green, executive director, Social Progress Imperative.
Description: Broomall, PA : Mason Crest, 2017. | Series: Social progress and sustainability | Includes index.
Identifiers: LCCN 2016007616| ISBN 9781422234990 (hardback) | ISBN 9781422234907 (series) | ISBN 9781422283943 (ebook)
Subjects: LCSH: Social indicators—South America—Juvenile literature. | South America—Social conditions—Juvenile literature. | South America—Economic conditions—Juvenile literature.
Classification: LCC HN254 .B68 2017 | DDC 306.098—dc23
LC record available at http://lccn.loc.gov/2016007616

Developed and Produced by Print Matters Productions, Inc. (www.printmattersinc.com)

Project Editor: David Andrews
Design: Bill Madrid, Madrid Design
Copy Editor: Laura Daly

Note on Statistics:
All social progress statistics, except where noted, are used by courtesy of the Social Progress Imperative and reflect 2015 ratings.

CONTENTS

KEY ICONS TO LOOK FOR:

Text-Dependent Questions: These questions send readers back to the text for more careful attention to the evidence presented there.

Words to Understand: These words with their easy-to-understand definitions will increase readers' understanding of the text while building vocabulary skills.

Series Glossary of Key Terms: This back-of-the-book glossary contains terminology used throughout this series. Words found here increase readers' ability to read and comprehend higher-level books and articles in this field.

Research Projects: Readers are pointed toward areas of further inquiry connected to each chapter. Suggestions are provided for projects that encourage deeper research and analysis.

Sidebars: This boxed material within the main text allows readers to build knowledge, gain insights, explore possibilities, and broaden their perspectives by weaving together additional information to provide realistic and holistic perspectives.

Michael Green
Executive Director
Social Progress Imperative

SOCIAL PROGRESS AROUND THE GLOBE

Michael Green

How do you measure the success of a country? It's not as easy as you might think.

Americans are used to thinking of their country as the best in the world, but what does "best" actually mean? For a long time, the United States performed better than any other country in terms of the sheer size of its economy, and bigger was considered better. Yet China caught up with the United States in 2014 and now has a larger overall economy.

What about average wealth? The United States does far better than China here but not as well as several countries in Europe and the Middle East.

Most of us would like to be richer, but is money really what we care about? Is wealth really how we want to measure the success of countries—or cities, neighborhoods, families, and individuals? Would you really want to be rich if it meant not having access to the World Wide Web, or suffering a painful disease, or not being safe when you walked near your home?

Using money to compare societies has a long history, including the invention in the 1930s of an economic measurement called gross domestic product (GDP). Basically, GDP for the United States "measures the output of goods and services produced by labor and property located within the U.S. during a given time period." The concept of GDP was actually created by the economist Simon Kuznets for use by the federal government. Using measures like GDP to guide national economic policies helped pull the United States out of the Great Depression and helped Europe and Japan recover after World War II. As they say in business school, if you can measure it, you can manage it.

Many positive activities contribute to GDP, such as

- Building schools and roads
- Growing crops and raising livestock
- Providing medical care

More and more experts, however, are seeing that we may need another way to measure the success of a nation.

Other kinds of activities increase a country's GDP, but are these signs that a country is moving in a positive direction?

- Building and maintaining larger prisons for more inmates
- Cleaning up after hurricanes or other natural disasters
- Buying alcohol and illegal drugs
- Maintaining ecologically unsustainable use of water, harvesting of trees, or catching of fish

GDP also does not address inequality. A few people could become extraordinarily wealthy, while the rest of a country is plunged into poverty and hunger, but this wouldn't be reflected in the GDP.

In the turbulent 1960s, Robert F. Kennedy, the attorney general of the United States and brother of President John F. Kennedy, famously said of GDP during a 1968 address to students at the University of Kansas: "It counts napalm and counts nuclear warheads and armored cars for the police to fight the riots in our cities ... [but] the gross national product does not allow for the health of our children.... [I]t measures everything in short, except that which makes life worthwhile."

For countries like the United States that already have large or strong economies, it is not clear that simply making the economy larger will improve human welfare. Developed countries struggle with issues like obesity, diabetes, crime, and environmental challenges. Increasingly, even poorer countries are struggling with these same issues.

Noting the difficulties that many countries experience as they grow wealthier (such as increased crime and obesity), people around the world have begun to wonder: What if we measure the things we really care about directly, rather than assuming that greater GDP will mean improvement in everything we care about? Is that even possible?

The good news is that it is. There is a new way to think about prosperity, one that does not depend on measuring economic activity using traditional tools like GDP.

Advocates of the "Beyond GDP" movement, people ranging from university professors to leaders of businesses, from politicians to religious leaders, are calling for more attention to directly measuring things we all care about, such as hunger, homelessness, disease, and unsafe water.

One of the new tools that has been developed is called the Social Progress Index (SPI), and it is the data from this index that is featured in this series of books, Social Progress and Sustainability.

The SPI has been created to measure and advance social progress outcomes at a fine level of detail in communities of different sizes and at different levels of wealth. This means that we can compare the performance of very different countries using one standard set of measurements, to get a sense of how well different countries perform compared to each other. The index measures how the different parts of society, including governments, businesses, not-for-profits, social entrepreneurs, universities, and colleges, work together to improve human welfare. Similarly, it does not strictly measure the actions taken in a particular place. Instead, it measures the outcomes in a place.

The SPI begins by defining what it means to be a good society, structured around three fundamental themes:

- Do people have the basic needs for survival: food, water, shelter, and safety?
- Do people have the building blocks of a better future: education, information, health, and sustainable ecosystems?

- Do people have a chance to fulfill their dreams and aspirations by having rights and freedom of choice, without discrimination, with access to the cutting edge of human knowledge?

The Social Progress Index is published each year, using the best available data for all the countries covered. You can explore the data on our website at http://socialprogressimperative.org. The data for this series of books is from our 2015 index, which covered 133 countries. Countries that do not appear in the 2015 index did not have the right data available to be included.

A few examples will help illustrate how overall Social Progress Index scores compare to measures of economic productivity (for example, GDP per capita), and also how countries can differ on specific lenses of social performance.

- The United States (6th for GDP per capita, 16th for SPI overall) ranks 6th for Shelter but 68th in Health and Wellness, because of factors such as obesity and death from heart disease.
- South Africa (62nd for GDP per capita, 63rd for SPI) ranks 44th in Access to Information and Communications but only 114th in Health and Wellness, because of factors such as relatively short life expectancy and obesity.
- India (93rd for GDP per capita, 101st for SPI) ranks 70th in Personal Rights but only 128th in Tolerance and Inclusion, because of factors such as low tolerance for different religions and low tolerance for homosexuals.
- China (66th for GDP per capita, 92nd for SPI) ranks 58th in Shelter but 84th in Water and Sanitation, because of factors such as access to piped water.
- Brazil (55th for GDP per capita, 42nd for SPI) ranks 61st in Nutrition and Basic Medical Care but only 122nd in Personal Safety, because of factors such as a high homicide rate.

The Social Progress Index focuses on outcomes. Politicians can boast that the government has spent millions on feeding the hungry; the SPI measures how well fed people really are. Businesses can boast investing money in their operations or how many hours their employees have volunteered in the community; the SPI measures actual literacy rates and access to the Internet. Legislators and administrators might focus on how much a country spends on health care; the SPI measures how long and how healthily people live. The index doesn't measure whether countries have passed laws against discrimination; it measures whether people experience discrimination. And so on.

- What if your family measured its success only by the amount of money it brought in but ignored the health and education of members of the family?
- What if a neighborhood focused only on the happiness of the majority while discriminating against one family because they were different?
- What if a country focused on building fast cars but was unable to provide clean water and air?

The Social Progress Index can also be adapted to measure human well-being in areas smaller than a whole country.

- A Social Progress Index for the Amazon region of Brazil, home to 24 million people and covering one of the world's most precious environmental assets, shows how 800 different municipalities compare. A map of that region shows where needs are greatest and is informing a development strategy for the region that balances the interests of people and the planet. Nonprofits, businesses, and governments in Brazil are now using this data to improve the lives of the people living in the Amazon region.
- The European Commission—the governmental body that manages the European Union—is using the Social Progress Index to compare the performance of multiple regions in each of 28 countries and to inform development strategies.
- We envision a future where the Social Progress Index will be used by communities of different sizes around the world to measure how well they are performing and to help guide governments, businesses, and nonprofits to make better choices about what they focus on improving, including learning lessons from other communities of similar size and wealth that may be performing better on some fronts. Even in the United States subnational social progress indexes are underway to help direct equitable growth for communities.

The Social Progress Index is intended to be used along with economic measurements such as GDP, which have been effective in guiding decisions that have lifted hundreds of millions of people out of abject poverty. But it is designed to let countries go even further, not just making economies larger but helping them devote resources to where they will improve social progress the most. The vision of my organization, the Social Progress Imperative, which created the Social Progress Index, is that in the future the Social Progress Index will be considered alongside GDP when people make decisions about how to invest money and time.

Imagine if we could measure what charities and volunteers really contribute to our societies. Imagine if businesses competed based on their whole contribution to society—not just economic, but social and environmental. Imagine if our politicians were held accountable for how much they made people's lives better, in real, tangible ways. Imagine if everyone, everywhere, woke up thinking about how their community performed on social progress and about what they could do to make it better.

Note on Text:
While Michael Green wrote the foreword and data is from the 2015 Social Progress Index, the rest of the text is not by Michael Green or the Social Progress Imperative.

This political map shows the countries of the region discussed in this book.

SOCIAL PROGRESS IN SOUTH AMERICA

From the subpolar region of Tierra del Fuego in the south, to the vast central basin of the Amazon River drainage, the great highlands of the Andes Mountains in the west, the steamy jungles that span both sides of the equator, and the white Caribbean beaches in the north, South America is a continent of great diversity, abundant natural resources, and stunning beauty. South Americans share a dramatic history of rich civilizations lost to European conquest in the 1500s. They survived the often cruel treatment from their conquerors only to face further violence at the hands of military dictatorships that took control in many countries after winning independence. Today the continent enjoys relative political stability and economic growth, but some countries suffer from uncontrolled crime, violence, and corruption.

This volume explores the level of social progress in the 12 countries of South America today. Social progress is a society's ability to meet the basic human needs of its citizens, create the building blocks that individuals and communities use to improve the quality of their lives, and make it possible for everyone to reach their potential. The book examines bare necessities, such as people's access to food, water, shelter, and basic medical care; it also considers whether people are safe, receive education, and enjoy personal freedom. It considers as well the political and natural environment.

To understand how social progress differs from one country to another, the Social Progress Imperative scored 133 countries around the world in three main areas:

Basic Human Needs: *Does a country provide for its people's most essential needs?*

Foundations of Well-being: *Are the building blocks in place for individuals and communities to enhance and sustain well-being?*

Opportunity: *Is there opportunity for all individuals to reach their full potential?*

Based on dozens of scores in these three areas, the Social Progress Imperative calculated an overall Social Progress Index (SPI) score for each country. Scores were then classified into six groups, from very low social progress to very high. As shown below, 11 of the 12 South American countries fell into the middle and high categories. (Note: Suriname was not included because some data were not available.) Actual scores for each country can be found in Chapter 4.

High Social Progress: *Uruguay and Chile*

Upper Middle Social Progress: *Argentina, Brazil, Colombia, Ecuador, Peru, and Paraguay*

Lower Middle Social Progress: *Venezuela, Bolivia, and Guyana*

Countries in South America and around the world are using SPI scores and rankings to identify areas for improvement and to help guide social investment. Even cities will soon be able to evaluate and compare their levels of social progress as the Social Progress Initiative releases more city-level scores like those recently published for 10 cities in Colombia (socialprogressimperative.org/data/spi/countries/COL).

Activists take to the streets of Lima, Peru, in advance of general elections.

The chapters that follow explore some of the stories behind the scores and look at some of the reasons for countries' strengths and weaknesses. You'll see how wealth and social progress are not always related and how a high score doesn't necessarily mean that all citizens share equally in that progress.

A Paraguayan peasant cooks in a square in the center of Asunción, Paraguay, during a grassroots demonstration calling on the Paraguayan government to cease forcible ejections of squatters from rural estates.

CHAPTER 1

BASIC HUMAN NEEDS

Words to Understand

Favela: a slum in or near a city in Brazil. Favelas are overcrowded and lack basic services.

GDP per capita (per person): the gross domestic product divided by the number of people in the country. For example, if the GDP for a country is one hundred million dollars ($100,000,000) and the population is one million people (1,000,000), then the GDP per capita (value created per person is $100).

Income inequality: when the wealth of a country is spread very unevenly among the population.

Nongovernmental organization (NGO): a nonprofit, voluntary citizens' group organized on a local, national, or international level. Examples include organizations that support human rights, advocate for political participation, and work for improved health care.

Undernourishment: not getting enough food or good-quality food to promote health or proper growth.

Basic human needs are the things that people need to live: enough food, clean water, improved sanitation, adequate shelter, and access to basic medical care. People also need to be safe and to feel safe. In 1948 the United Nations adopted the Universal Declaration of Human Rights as a shared standard for all people in all countries. Article 25 of the declaration says:

Everyone has the right to a standard of living adequate for the health and well-being of himself and of his family, including food, clothing, housing and medical care and necessary social services, and the right to security in the event of unemployment, sickness, disability, widowhood, old age or other lack of livelihood in circumstances beyond his control.

All 12 countries in South America agreed to this statement, promising to promote social progress and better standards of living for their citizens. To see how well each country is doing in providing for the most basic of human needs, the Social Progress Imperative scored 133 countries around the world in four categories:

Water and Sanitation: *Can people drink the water without getting sick?*
Nutrition and Basic Medical Care: *Do people have enough to eat? Can they see a doctor?*
Shelter: *Do people have housing with basic utilities, such as electricity?*
Personal Safety: *Are people safe from violence? Do they feel afraid?*

The following table shows the South American countries with the two highest and the two lowest overall scores, along with their rankings among the 133 SPI countries.

	CHILE #1 in SA	URUGUAY #2 in SA	BOLIVIA #10 in SA	VENEZUELA #11* in SA
	Score (Rank)	Score (Rank)	Score (Rank)	Score (Rank)
GDP per capita**	**$21,714 (40th)**	**$18,966 (42nd)**	**$5,934 (90th)**	**$17,615 (46th)**
Nutrition/medical	**97.84 (43rd)**	**97.57 (49th)**	**81.12 (97th)**	**95.99 (65th)**
Water/sanitation	**95.23 (40th)**	**96.33 (36th)**	**65.02 (91st)**	**81.86 (67th)**
Shelter	**80.00 (36th)**	**78.70 (39th)**	**61.38 (85th)**	**61.02 (86th)**
Personal safety	**72.19 (40th)**	**72.11 (41st)**	**61.46 (70th)**	**25.59 (131st)**
Overall Basic Needs	**86.32 (35th)**	**86.18 (37th)**	**67.24 (85th)**	**66.12 (87th)**

Source: Social Progress Index (SPI).

* Only 11 of the 12 countries were ranked; Suriname could not be included because of missing data in some categories.

** Gross domestic product (GDP) is the total value of all products and services created in a country during a year. GDP per capita (per person) is the gross domestic product divided by the number of people in the country. The GDP ranking shown is the rank among the 133 SPI countries.

The red and blue numbers in the table show a relationship between income and social progress. Chile and Uruguay are two of the richest countries in South America, so it's not surprising that they are the top scorers. What's more, the blue scores show that both countries do a better job at providing shelter than do other countries around the world with similar economies. Uruguay's overall score is also higher than would be expected if money were the only factor in achieving social progress.

A fruit seller meets others' needs and her own in the old city of Cartagena, Colombia.

At the other end of the scale, the red scores highlight where another high-income country has the worst performance in South America in meeting the basic needs of its people. Venezuela's GDP per capita of more than $17,000 is almost as high as Uruguay's, yet it underperforms even Bolivia (South America's poorest country) in the categories of Shelter and Personal Safety. Other countries that showed relatively weak performance against others in the same income brackets were Brazil, Colombia, and Ecuador.

Income inequality is when most of a country's wealth is held by a small percentage of the population. It plays a role in lower SPI scores, even in rich countries. Oxfam (oxfam.org), a charity that fights poverty, estimates that the richest 1 percent of the world's population has more wealth than the other 99 percent combined.

Unfair social treatment and unequal protection under the law also add to the number of people whose basic needs don't get met. Groups especially vulnerable to these kinds of social injustices are the poor, the elderly, children, women, immigrants, racial minorities, and refugees.

Nutrition and Basic Medical Care

Undernourishment has many causes, including rising food prices with no increase in wages, poverty, unemployment, an unstable economy, trade imbalances, and dependence on imports. Those without money for healthy, good food buy cheaper, less nutritious foods instead. More than 10 percent of the population is malnourished in five South American countries. These countries also have a high percentage of people living outside the cities in **rural areas**.

	Country	% Undernourished	% Rural
	Bolivia	19.5	32
	Colombia	11.4	24
	Ecuador	11.2	36
	Paraguay	11.0	41
	Guyana	10.0	72

Nearly 2 out of every 10 people and 1 out of every 3 children in Bolivia don't get enough calories each day. Bolivia ranks 108th of the 133 countries listed on the SPI. Largely due to undernourishment, child and maternal mortality rates in Bolivia are the second highest in the hemisphere. A country's maternal mortality rate is how many pregnant women die for every 100,000 births, and the child mortality rate is how many children die before their fifth birthday for every 1,000 born.

According to the World Bank, unequal access to health care is the number one killer of mother and children. Most doctors, clinics, and hospitals are located in cities. People who live in rural areas are often poor and can't afford to go into town for treatment. They often die from diseases that could have been prevented or cured with basic medical care.

Food Fads in North America and Europe Hurt South Americans

Quinoa is a nutritious seed that originated in the Andes Mountains of South America. Quinoa seed is high in vitamins and minerals and provides complete protein. It's an important part of people's diet in Bolivia and Peru. Recently, quinoa has captured the attention of the health food industry in Europe and North America. It's now sold to wealthy consumers as an organic, gluten-free, vegan, "miracle" food.

Because of the increased outside demand for quinoa, farmers can make a lot more money selling their crop to foreign corporations than to their poor neighbors. The local people who used to eat quinoa to stay alive can no longer afford to buy it. In some areas, quinoa now costs more than chicken.

An indigenous woman of the Aymara people carries quinoa in Huatajata, Bolivia. For centuries Bolivians have grown quinoa, a highly nutritious seed. The harvest of this cereal typical of the Andean region takes place in June, before the arrival of the winter.

Water and Sanitation

Contaminated water and poor sanitation spread diseases such as diarrhea, cholera, typhoid, hepatitis, dengue fever, polio, and malaria. These diseases are often a death sentence for people who don't have access to vaccines that prevent disease and medical care. The table below shows the highest and lowest scores in South America in the Water and Sanitation category.

	ARGENTINA Score (Rank)	URUGUAY Score (Rank)	PERU Score (Rank)	BOLIVIA Score (Rank)
Water and sanitation	**96.56 (35th)**	**96.33 (36th)**	**73.11 (86th)**	**73.02 (91st)**

More than 99 percent of the people in Uruguay and 98 percent in Chile and Argentina have access to piped water (water delivered through a pipe to their home or property). Only 67 percent of the people in Suriname and Guyana have piped water, the lowest access on the continent.

Guyana has the best rural access to improved water sources in South America, with almost 98 percent of residents having access. In Peru and Bolivia only about 72 percent of the rural population has access to safe water. Ecuador, Peru, and Venezuela all showed room for improvement in this category.

Only about 8 out of 10 Peruvians have piped water. In the city, tankers deliver water for people's daily needs.

If you live in Chile or Argentina, you are two times more likely to have improved sanitation facilities than if you live in Bolivia. In Bolivia only about 46 percent of the people have the kind of sanitary facility that separates human waste from human contact. Brazil, Ecuador, Peru, and Suriname all showed a relative weakness in this category when compared to other countries with similar economies.

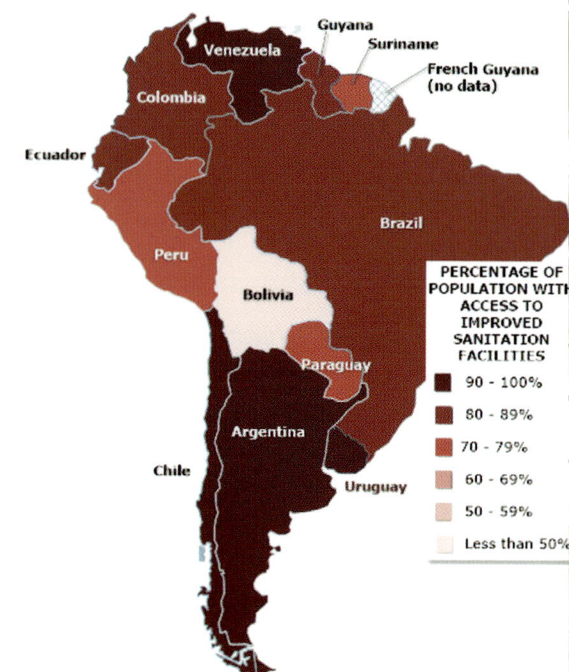

Shelter

People need adequate shelter with reliable power for cooking, heating, and lighting to keep them safe and healthy. Many people in South America cook indoors on open wood fires that pollute the air with smoke, which causes lung infections and cancer. In Bolivia almost 7 out of every 10 houses have dirt floors, which also can contribute to lung diseases and other illnesses.

Access to electricity is close to 100 percent in Venezuela, Suriname, Chile, and Uruguay. In Bolivia only 80 percent of the people have access, and in Guyana only 77 percent do. The quality of electricity is poor in Guyana, Argentina, and Peru.

In the Andes, the guinea pigs that people raise for food are kept loose in the house.

When people in South America were asked whether they were "satisfied or dissatisfied with the availability of good, affordable housing" where they live, most said that they were dissatisfied. Only 52 percent of Ecuadorians reported being satisfied. In every other country less than 50% were satisfied, with the least satisfied groups in Venezuela (35 percent) and Uruguay (28 percent).

Housing Crisis in Brazil

A favela on the outskirts of São Paulo, Brazil. More than one million São Paulo residents live in favelas.

Brazil needs between 6 and 8 million more houses than it has. The biggest need is for low-income housing for the poor. Brazil's two largest cities, São Paulo and Rio de Janeiro, are among the most expensive in the world. The cost of buying an apartment in these cities is more than $400 per square foot.

The cities of Brazil are surrounded by informal settlements called **favelas**. Favelas don't usually have clean water, sanitation, or trash collection. Crime, gang violence, and clashes with police are common. Most people living in these slums earn less than the minimum wage of $300 per month and have nowhere else to go.

Personal Safety

South America can be a dangerous place. In 2012 one in five murder victims in the world was Brazilian, Colombian, or Venezuelan. According to the SPI, people in Brazil, Venezuela, Guyana, Colombia, and Peru think it is likely that violent crime will pose a problem for businesses or government in 2016–2017. In half of South American countries, people have high or very high distrust of their fellow citizens. Only five countries—Chile, Uruguay, Peru, Bolivia, and Argentina—topped the average world score of 56.27 for Personal Safety. Brazil (35.55) and Venezuela (25.59) had the worst scores in South America. Of the other 133 SPI countries, only Nigeria and Iran had lower scores than Venezuela. The table below shows all the rankings related to safety for Brazil and Venezuela.

	BRAZIL World Rank	VENEZUELA World Rank
Murder rate	113th	113th
Violent crime	105th	105th
Political terror	119th	109th
Perceived criminality	94th	123rd
Traffic deaths	105th	129th
Overall Personal Safety	122nd	131st

Brazilians' high distrust of their fellow citizens and their lack of faith in the ability of the police to protect them (perceived criminality) stem from the fact that only 92 to 95 percent of murders go unsolved in Brazil. Recent investments in law enforcement have improved the situation in Brazilian cities, but murder rates continue to increase everywhere else.

In Venezuela a declining economy based on oil and increasing social unrest have made it difficult for the government to control criminal and police violence across the country. The Venezuelan government doesn't release crime statistics, but the Venezuelan Violence Observatory, a **nongovernmental organization** (NGO) made up of researchers from seven Venezuelan universities, estimates that there were 27,875 murders in 2015, making it one of the most violent countries in the world. Only 10 percent of murderers in Venezuela get caught.

People in Ecuador, Guyana, Uruguay, and Brazil are almost twice as likely to die in a car accident as people in Argentina, Chile, or the United States. The odds of dying are even higher in Venezuela, which ranks 129th of 133 countries in the number of traffic deaths.

The number of traffic deaths in Guyana is among the highest in the world. It ranks 120th of 133.

Text-Dependent Questions

1. Income inequality is when most of a country's wealth is held by a small percentage of the population. Why does income inequality hurt social progress?
2. Why is it more difficult for rural residents to get basic medical care than it is for those in cities?
3. Which country in South America is the most dangerous?
4. List three causes of the high murder rates in Venezuela and Brazil.
5. Name two ways that inadequate shelter can lead to lung diseases.

Research Project

With the help of your teacher, organize a research project to find out how safe students feel at your school. You'll conduct a survey of each grade and compare and rank the results.

1. Prepare a survey for the students that looks like the one below. Make copies for every student you plan to ask. (Don't ask students for their names. The survey should be anonymous.)

> 1. Read the statement below and then check the box that best describes your level of agreement.
>
>   *I feel safe when I am at school.*
>
>   ☐ **Strongly no** ☐ **No** ☐ **Yes** ☐ **Strongly yes**
>
> 2. Please write your grade in the space provided and circle your gender.
>
>   Grade ___________ Gender (circle one) **M** **F**

2. Work with your teacher to decide when and where to hand out the surveys. When you have the completed surveys, separate them into grades. Assign the following values to each answer: Strongly no = 1 point, No = 2 points, Yes = 3 points, Strongly yes = 4 points.
3. Count the number of surveys for one grade, and add up the total number of points, then divide by the number of surveys to get an average score. For a grade with 30 surveys returned, for example, the calculation might look like this:

5 surveys @ 1 point	=	5 points
8 surveys @ 2 points	=	16 points
7 surveys @ 3 points	=	21 points
10 surveys @ 4 points	=	40 points
Total points =		82 points divided by 30 surveys = 2.73 average score

   The score of 2.73 shows that not everyone in this grade feels safe. What would an average score of 4 tell you? An average score of 2?
4. Repeat the process for the other grades you surveyed.
5. Compare the scores of each grade. Rank the grades, with number 1 being the grade with the highest score. Do students in some grades feel safer than others? Do some grades feel very unsafe?
6. Next, add all the scores of surveys completed by males in every grade. Divide by the total number of male surveys to get the average score for males. Do the same for females.

7. Compare the scores for the males and females. Is there a big difference between the scores?
8. Present your results to your class. If there are differences in the scores for the various grades or in the scores for males and females, lead a discussion to get ideas about what might explain these differences.

Ashaninka boy with face painted using the reddish seeds of the urucum plant enjoys an afternoon with his mother in the state of Acre, Brazil.

Chapter 2

Foundations of Well-being

Words to Understand

Adult literacy rate: the percentage of adults (generally defined as those age 15 and older) who can read and write.

Deforestation: the cutting down or clearing of trees with no intention of replanting.

Ecosystem sustainability: when we care for resources like clean air, water, plants, and animals so that they will be available to future generations.

Indigenous people: culturally distinct groups with long-standing ties to the land in a specific area. Estimates are that 23 million indigenous people inhabited what is now South America when European settlers first arrived.

Nongovernmental organization (NGO): a nonprofit, voluntary citizens' group organized on a local, national, or international level. Examples include organizations that support human rights, advocate for political participation, and work for improved health care.

Real social progress goes further than simply having the basics to stay alive. People also need to be educated and allowed to develop the skills that will help them improve the quality of their lives. They need an environment that gives them a sense of well-being, an environment that makes them feel comfortable, healthy, and happy.

To compare how well countries around the world were providing the building blocks that citizens and communities use to create better lives, the Social Progress Imperative looked at 133 countries in four areas:

Access to Basic Knowledge: *Can children go to school? Can adults read and write?*

Access to Information and Communications: *Do people have Internet access? Cell phones? Is the news they hear and read controlled by the government or special interests?*

Health and Wellness: *How long do people live? Do they die early from treatable diseases?*

Ecosystem Sustainability: *Will future generations live in a healthy environment?*

The average score for South American countries in Foundations of Well-being was 73.33, about 8 percent higher than the world average of 67.68. The table below compares the rank of each country's economy with its rank in providing the Foundations of Well-being for its citizens.

		GDP per Capita* World Rank (of 133)	Foundations of Well-being World Rank (of 133)
	Chile	40	38
	Uruguay	42	**36**
	Venezuela	46	41
	Brazil	55	**30**
	Colombia	63	**23**
	Peru	68	**45**
	Ecuador	71	**28**
	Paraguay	80	59
	Guyana	88	**104**
	Bolivia	90	**30**
	Argentina	Unranked	47
	Suriname	Unranked	Unranked

Source: Social Progress Index.

* Gross domestic product (GDP) is the total dollar value of all products and services created in a country during a year. GDP per capita (per person) is the gross domestic product divided by the number of people in the country. The GDP ranking shown is the rank among the 133 SPI countries.

The SPI scores show many good efforts in South America and also room for improvement across the four categories used to calculate the overall well-being score. Most countries ranked higher in Foundations of Well-being than in GDP per capita. The numbers in blue highlight the countries that scored higher than other countries with similar economies. Half of the South American countries rank in the top one-third of the world in providing the Foundations of Well-being. Bolivia, Brazil, Colombia, Ecuador, Peru, and Uruguay all performed better than their economic equals. The only country that underperformed consistently compared to other countries with similar wealth was Guyana, which was also the lowest-ranking country in South America and ranked in the bottom 25 percent of countries, at 104th.

SPI scores show that it's not always the richest countries that have the best scores. In addition to money, social progress requires the will of the people and the support of the government. Uruguay has the second-largest GDP per capita in South America and the highest overall score in providing the foundations of well-being. It also scored higher than other countries with similar economies. Why? One reason is surely the example set by José Mujica, the president of Uruguay from 2010 to 2015. During his time as president, Mujica showed his support for social progress by giving 90 percent of his $12,000 per month salary to charities that help the poor and small businesses.

Access to Basic Knowledge

A primary school student in class at the Fatima school in Montevideo, Uruguay.

A basic education is necessary to achieve social progress in any country. Education and poverty are linked. Poor people are often uneducated. Children of uneducated parents learn less at home and have fewer opportunities to go to school, which creates a cycle of poverty that continues from one generation to the next.

Education, Rural Populations, and Poverty

Poor children who live in rural areas have even less access to education than poor children who live in urban areas. Rural areas have fewer people to cover the cost of building schools and hiring teachers. Houses are spread out, and people often don't have transportation to attend a centrally located school. In many villages along the Amazon River, the only access to other communities is by boat. The effects of a large rural population on Access to Basic Knowledge scores is suggested in the following table:

Country	Access to Basic Knowledge	% Rural	Estimated % Poverty	South America Rank (of 12)
Brazil	**96.13**	**14**	**21%**	**1**
Uruguay	**95.54**	**5**	**19%**	**2**
Argentina	**95.29**	**8**	**30%**	**3**
Bolivia	**87.50**	**31**	**45%**	**10**
Guyana	**87.27**	**73**	**35%**	**11**
Paraguay	**83.25**	**40**	**35%**	**12**

As in other regions of the world, leaders in South America recognize the need to improve education levels, beginning with primary education, or elementary school. But high rates of poverty continue to keep too many children out of classrooms. In Bolivia, for example, only 84 of every 100 children who should be in primary school are enrolled, which puts it at a low rank of 104th of 133 countries. Not only does Bolivia have a large rural population, but 45 percent of the people live below the international poverty line, which is less than $2 per day. The rates of access to secondary education (US middle and high school) are even worse. Paraguay, for instance, ranks a low 104th in lower secondary school enrollment, and at 114th, Guyana ranks lowest in upper secondary school enrollment.

Most South American countries need to help poor children get in school and stay in school. There is a high dropout rate in South American countries. According to Worldfund (worldfund.org), only 41 percent of Brazilian students go on to graduate from secondary schools. Children from lower-income families complete an average of 8 years of school, compared to more than 10 years for children in upper-income families. Help could take the form of hiring more and better teachers, building more schools, and helping families pay for uniforms, books, and transportation. Older students might be helped by work-study programs that allow them to help support their families.

Adult literacy rate

Low school enrollments result in lower **adult literacy rates**. The following chart shows the literacy rates for the countries in South America.

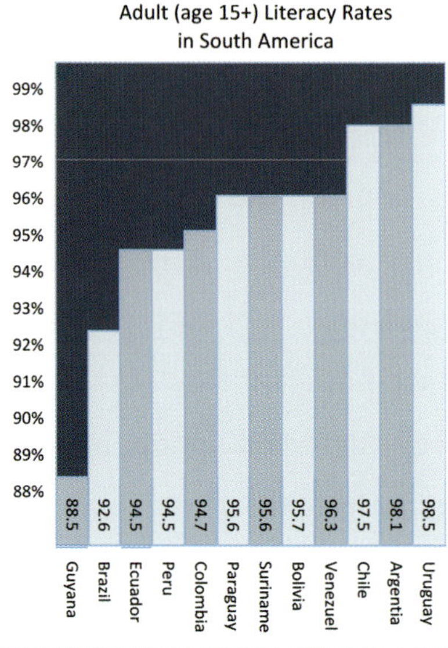

NOTE: INFOGRAPHIC (WORD TABLE) BY AUTHOR BASED ON CIA FACTBOOK DATA.

Access to Information and Communications

Cell phones and Internet access have become important tools for getting information. People need information they can trust so they can make good decisions and stay safe. The SPI scores in this category show the level of freedom that people have to access information and ideas.

Argentina, Brazil, Chile, Colombia, and Ecuador all have more than one cell phone subscription per citizen. Guyana has only 61 cell phones per 100 people, a relative weakness compared to other countries with similar wealth.

Internet by the hour in Colombia—Biblioteca Piloto del Caribe Sala de Internet y Multimedia, Barranquilla, Atlántico.

South American countries have about the same amount of Internet use as people in other countries with similar economies. Only Suriname shows a relative weakness, with about 37 percent of its citizens having Internet connections. The table below shows the highest and lowest scores in South America in these categories.

	#1 in SA	#2 in SA	#11 in SA	#12 in SA
Cell phone subscriptions per 100 people	Argentina (159)	Brazil (135)	Paraguay (70)	Guyana (61)
Population using the Internet	Chile (66%)	Argentina (59%)	Paraguay (36%)	Guyana (33%)

Press Freedom Index

As part of the Access to Information and Communications score, the Social Progress Imperative used the Press Freedom Index. (In journalism, the press are the news media companies and the people who work for them.) The index is created each year by Reporters Without Borders (rsf.org), a nonprofit, **nongovernmental organization** that promotes freedom of information and freedom of the press. Index scores are based on four main categories:

Fairness of the news media (print, broadcast, and online): *Are both sides of a story told? Are all cultural and political groups treated fairly in the news?*

Independence of news media: *Are most of the news outlets owned by the government or by just a few companies that control what people read and hear?*

Level of respect for the safety/freedom of journalists: *Do reporters face violence or jail for doing their jobs?*

Working environment for the news media: *Do the laws protect journalists? Are the media afraid of the government? Organized crime? Terrorists?*

In 2014 Reporters Without Borders classified the freedom of the press in South American countries as follows:

Good Situation →	**No countries**
Satisfactory Situation→	Suriname, Uruguay
Noticeable Problems→	Argentina, Brazil, Bolivia*, Chile, Ecuador*, Guyana, Paraguay , Peru
Difficult Situation→	Colombia, Venezuela
Very Serious Situation→	No countries

*Showed significant improvement over the previous year.

Colombia is the second-most-dangerous country in the Americas (includes North, Central, and South America) for journalists, after Mexico. Reporters there face threats, imprisonment, and violence when they write stories about people who use their positions of power for personal gain, expose the activities of groups who work together to break the law (organized crime), or publish stories about those who violate people's human rights. From 2000 to 2013, more than 50 journalists were killed in Colombia. During the same period more than 350 journalists received threats, and in only one case were those responsible arrested.

Uruguay is at the other end of the press freedom scale. In 2013 Uruguay passed a law that showed that it values freedom of information. The law gives one-third of the country's radio licenses to community stations, one-third to commercial stations, and one-third to government-owned stations. The increase in the number of community-owned stations will allow people to get news and information about their communities instead of just news about the events in the big cities.

Health and Wellness

Every country has its own system of health care. All systems have the same goal, which is to provide health care for everyone and protect people from financial ruin from high medical bills. Argentina, Brazil, Chile, Colombia, Peru, Uruguay, and Paraguay all have universal health care, where everyone has health insurance under the same system. These systems are run by the government and paid for by the public through taxes.

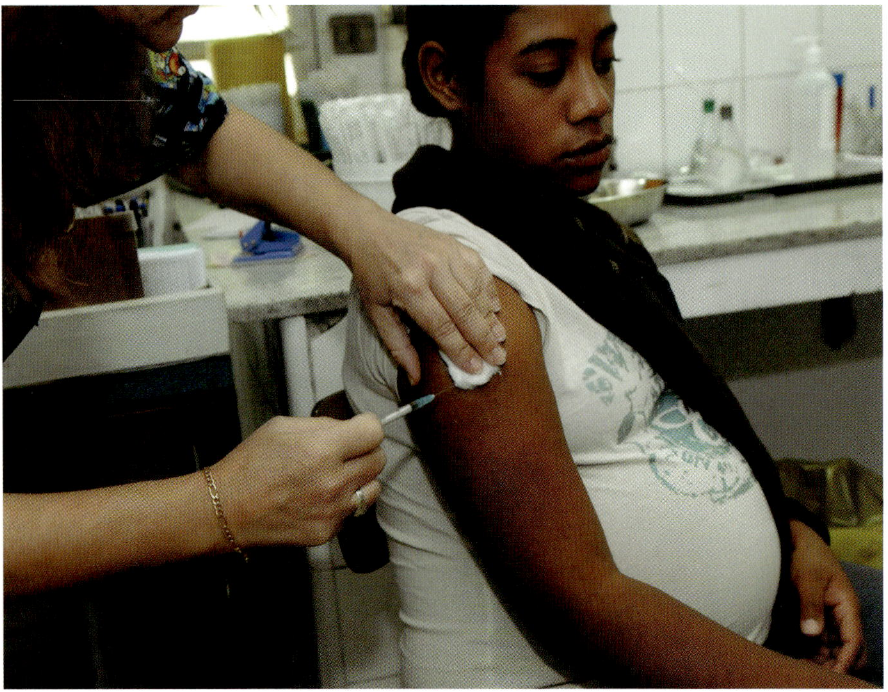

A pregnant woman takes an A/H1N1 vaccine in Montevideo, Uruguay, as part of a government vaccination program to prevent influenza in pregnant women, children, and elderly people.

Unfortunately, even when everyone has insurance, not everyone gets equal access to doctors and hospitals. Even in countries with universal health care, private health insurance is available to those who can pay for it. Private insurance means access to the best doctors, specialists, and hospitals.

Overall access to health care is lower in countries with large populations of native, or **indigenous, people**. In part, this is because many indigenous people live in rural areas. Bolivia and Ecuador both have large rural and large indigenous populations. In Bolivia 31 percent of the people live in rural areas, and 45 percent have no access to health care. Thirty-six percent of Ecuadorians live in rural areas, and 27 percent don't have health care.

The Health and Wellness score on the SPI was calculated by combining scores in these areas:

Deaths from outdoor air pollution *(fewest: Paraguay; most: Guyana)*
Life expectancy *(longest: 79.6 years in Chile; shortest: 66.0 years in Guyana)*
Suicide rate *(highest: Guyana; lowest: Peru)*
Obesity rate *(highest: Venezuela; lowest: Peru)*
Early deaths from preventable/treatable diseases *(fewest: Peru; most: Guyana)*

The top-ranking countries in South America for overall Health and Wellness were Peru and Colombia. The bottom-ranking countries were Suriname and Guyana.

Ecosystem Sustainability

If an activity is not sustainable, there will come a time when it's no longer possible to do it. For example, if you spend more money than you earn, that activity is not sustainable because at some point you will run out of money. **Ecosystem sustainability** is when we care for natural resources like clean air, water, plants, and animals in such a way that they will still be here for future generations. To measure ecosystem sustainability, the Social Progress Index compared countries in three categories: greenhouse gas emissions, water use, and protection of habitats and species. Unfortunately, companies doing business in countries that are rich in natural resources but have few regulations can earn huge profits at the expense of the environment.

The red-eyed tree frog and the toucan barbet are among the thousands of species in South America that are endangered due to pollution, hunting, fishing, collecting, and loss of habitat.

The top scores in ecosystem sustainability were earned by Colombia (world rank 18th) and Ecuador (world rank 31st). Bottom scores went to Argentina (world rank 89th) and Guyana (world rank 104th).

Biodiversity and habitat

Biodiversity is the variety of plant and animal life in an area. Habitat is the environment in which a plant or animal lives. Brazil has the most biodiversity of any country in the world. It has the most species of mammals and fish and is home to more than 50,000 species of trees and bushes. Colombia and Ecuador are also listed among the top 10 countries in biodiversity. Venezuela, Ecuador, and Bolivia had the top SPI scores for protecting their biodiversity and habitats. Low scores went to Guyana, Uruguay, and Paraguay.

Even with some countries working hard to protect land and ocean areas, as of 2015, South America had almost 6,000 threatened species, as shown in the table below.

	Mammals	Birds	Reptiles	Amphibians	Fish	Plants	Other	Total
Argentina	39	49	6	30	36	44	13	243
Bolivia	21	55	3	35	0	72	3	216
Brazil	81	164	29	36	86	386	54	966
Chile	20	32	2	22	22	49	12	182
Colombia	56	119	22	215	61	223	33	751
Ecuador	46	96	26	174	53	1835	65	2308
Guyana	11	14	5	5	28	22	1	87
Paraguay	9	27	3	0	0	10	0	58
Peru	55	121	9	111	21	276	4	643
Suriname	9	8	5	1	26	26	1	76
Uruguay	10	22	5	5	37	1	2	103
Venezuela	34	45	14	73	43	69	25	312

Source: IUCN Red List of Endangered Species

Greenhouse gas emissions

Gases that trap heat in earth's atmosphere are called greenhouse gases. Some of these gases are found naturally in the environment; others are released by the activities of humans. Carbon dioxide is the main greenhouse gas. It's released when people burn coal, natural gas, or oil. Plants absorb carbon dioxide, so when forests are cut or land is cleared for houses, even more carbon dioxide gets into the atmosphere.

Measuring greenhouse gas emissions is important because they have been linked to global warming and climate change. Global warming is expected to have a negative effect on the environment by increasing the average world temperature, which will change where and how much it rains and snows, reduce ice and snow cover, raise the sea level, and increase ocean acidity.

The four South American countries with the highest greenhouse emissions are Bolivia, Guyana, Paraguay, and Uruguay. Their high levels are due mostly to cutting down forests for agriculture. Family farmers and corporate growers cut down tropical forests to plant food for local populations and crops like soybeans for export to other countries. This tropical **deforestation** contributes greatly to greenhouse emissions and reduces biodiversity by killing off the plant and animal species that need the forests to live.

Unsustainable Agriculture: Slash and Burn

Tropical soil isn't fertile. Family farmers in the tropics burn forests to grow food because the ashes add nutrients to the soil. Then they can grow food in the burned area for a few years. After that the farmers must move to a new area and burn more forest. This practice is unsustainable because the burned land is good for growing food for only a short time, but it can take 50 years for a tropical forest to grow back.

Slash-and-burn forest clearing along the Xingu River in Brazil from space. The amount of carbon dioxide released into the atmosphere each year from tropical deforestation is more than is released by all the vehicles in the world combined.

Water stress

Ecosystem Sustainability was the category with the lowest scores in South America because of unsustainable use of water resources throughout the region. Seven of the 12 countries ranked lower in water stress than other countries with similar wealth. Water stress is measured by how much water a country has compared to how much it uses for all purposes, including for agriculture, industry, and personal use. Countries with medium, high, and extremely high water stress levels such as Peru and Chile need to work quickly to manage their water resources to avoid severe shortages in the near future.

Text-Dependent Questions

1. Name two ways that burning forests contributes to carbon dioxide emissions in South America.
2. Which South American country has the most biodiversity in the world?
3. Which country is the second-most-dangerous country in the Americas for journalists?
4. Name two reasons why it's harder for children in rural areas to get an education.
5. Who is José Mujica? What did he do that makes him an important role model?

Research Project

For this project, you will use an online water risk atlas developed by the World Resources Institute (WRI, wri.org). WRI is a global research organization that provides up-to-date information and expertise to help communities, businesses, and governments act in ways that improve people's lives and sustain a healthy environment. Follow the steps below to explore the current and future water-related risks in South America.

1. **Go to the Water Risk Atlas website:** *wri.org/resources/maps/aqueduct-water-risk-atlas.*
2. **Open the interactive map application:** Click the *LAUNCH THE INTERACTIVE MAP* link just above the world map.
3. **Explore water risk maps:** Select *Explore global water risk* maps by clicking on the magnifying glass icon.
4. **Look at current conditions:** Drag the map to center South America on the screen. Click the *Current Conditions* tab in the upper left corner.
5. **Explore the map:** Use the legend in the upper right corner to understand the current water risks across the continent.
6. **Explore future conditions:** Next, click the *Future Conditions* tab in the upper left corner. Use the new legend displayed in the upper right corner to learn how water risks are expected to change over time. Select different indicators, such as historical conditions or climate changes. Write one page on the findings you find most interesting.

Teachers and members of the student community rally through the streets of Quito, Ecuador, heading to Carondelet Palace, where the country's vice president met with education union delegates.

CHAPTER 3

OPPORTUNITY

Words to Understand

Contraception: any form of birth control used to prevent pregnancy.

Corruption: the dishonest behavior by people in positions of power for their own benefit.

Inflation: when the same amount of money buys less from one day to the next. Just because things cost more does not mean that people have more money. Low-income people trapped in a high-inflation economy can quickly find themselves unable to purchase even the basics, like food.

Prejudice: an opinion that isn't based on facts or reason.

Stereotypes: common beliefs about the nature of the members of a specific group that are based on limited experience or incorrect information.

To reach our potential, we need freedom and opportunity. We want the freedom to move around, practice our religions, and make our own choices. We want an equal opportunity to get a college degree and have a voice in the political process. To better understand how the level of opportunity differs from one country to another, the Social Progress Imperative scored 133 countries in the following categories:

Personal Freedom and Choice: *Are people allowed to make their own decisions?*

Tolerance and Inclusion: *Does everyone have the same opportunity to contribute?*

Access to Advanced Education: *Does everyone have the opportunity to go to college?*

Personal Rights: *Are people's individual rights restricted by the government?*

The average SPI Opportunity score of 60.07 in South America was more than eight points higher than the world average of 52.03. The table below shows the SPI scores and rankings in each category for the two highest- and two lowest-scoring South American countries.

	URUGUAY #1 in SA	**CHILE #2 in SA**	**GUYANA #11 in SA**	**VENEZUELA #12 in SA**
	Score (Rank)	**Score (Rank)**	**Score (Rank)**	**Score (Rank)**
GDP per capita*	$18,966 (42nd)	$21,714 (40th)	$6,336 (88th)	$17,615 (46th)
Freedom/choice	**82.56 (16th)**	**77.66 (22nd)**	55.42 (88th)	**54.35 (91st)**
Tolerance/inclusion	**84.12 (4th)**	**67.12 (22nd)**	55.32 (56th)	60.58 (39th)
Advanced education	**45.93 (69th)**	60.38 (31st)	37.21 (80th)	46.66 (67th)
Personal rights	**93.04 (6th)**	**89.60 (9th)**	59.63 (66th)	**36.60 (98th)**
Overall Opportunity	**76.41 (17th)**	**73.69 (21st)**	**51.89 (62nd)**	**49.55 (69th)**

Source: Social Progress Index

* Gross domestic product (GDP) is the total value of all products and services created in a country during a year. GDP per capita (per person) is the gross domestic product divided by the number of people in the country. The GDP ranking shown is the rank among the 133 SPI countries.

The red and blue numbers in the table show a relationship between income and social progress. Blue scores highlight where countries are doing a better job at providing opportunities than other countries around the world with similar economies. Red scores show where countries are not doing as well as their economic equals. Venezuela's GDP per capita of more than $17,000 is almost as high as Uruguay's, yet it scores lower in two categories than Guyana, which is one of the poorest countries.

Personal Freedom and Choice

Scores in the category of Personal Freedom and Choice help us to understand how much freedom citizens in each country have to make important decisions about things like religion, marriage, and children. It also considers the level of **corruption** because corruption limits everyone's freedom.

Demonstrators wave a gay pride flag outside Argentina's Congress in support of a successful proposal to legalize same sex marriage.

Eleven countries in South America scored very high in the Freedom of Religion category. Venezuela scored slightly lower, partly because of financial advantages given by the government to the Catholic Church.

Teen Marriage and Birth Control

Teen marriage makes it hard for young people to take advantage of whatever opportunities are available to them. Marriage before finishing high school can mean dropping out to get jobs. Early marriage for girls 15 to 18 years old often follows pregnancy. Child care can be expensive, so young mothers sometimes have to quit school to stay home with their children.

Pregnant teen beggar gets no special attention on the street in Venezuela.

More and more South American women use modern forms of **contraception** to limit the number of children they have. Eighty-seven percent of women who are married or in a committed relationship in Chile and Uruguay use contraception. Both countries have fewer early marriages than countries with low use of birth control. At 22 percent, Ecuador has the highest rate of early marriage in South America.

Freedom over life choices

Are you satisfied or dissatisfied with your freedom to choose what you do with your life? The table below shows how people in 11 South American countries answered that question.

Percent Satisfied	Country	(Rank of 133)
81–90	Paraguay	(19th)
	Suriname	(unranked*)
	Uruguay	(21st)
	Bolivia	(34th)
71–80	Colombia	(40th)
	Chile	(58th)
	Argentina	(61st)
	Ecuador	(64th)
	Brazil	(67th)
	Peru	(70th)
61–70	Guyana	(87th)
	Venezuela	(98th)

* Suriname was not ranked in the SPI because missing data made it impossible to compare it fairly to other countries.

Corruption

Corruption creates an unfair society that favors some people over others. When people in power take advantage of their positions for their own benefit, we say that they are corrupt or that there is corruption in the system. Corruption often takes the form of accepting money or favors (bribes) to break the rules or just to do the job they are already paid to do. The following table shows SPI corruption scores derived from data from Transparency International on how much corruption people think is happening in their country. The lower the score, the more corruption people believe there is.

Score	↑ LESS CORRUPTION / MORE CORRUPTION ↓	Country
81–100		(no countries)
71–80		Chile, Uruguay
51–70		(no countries)
41–50		Brazil
31–40		Guyana, Ecuador, Argentina, Bolivia, Suriname, Colombia, Peru
21–30		Paraguay
0–20		Venezuela

In Venezuela a weak economy, high **inflation**, and food shortages have created opportunities for corrupt individuals to take advantage of the situation. Another country with a high level of corruption is Paraguay. The situation there was so bad that Paraguay's president, Horacio Cartes, made a public demand for government officials to "stop robbing" the country. "Don't rob anymore. It's the people's money," he said.

Protest sign in Venezuela reads: "Why Do Venezuelans Protest? Insecurity, Violence, Injustice, Corruption, Shortages, Censorship. To protest is not a crime; it is a right."

Tolerance and Inclusion

Scores for Tolerance and Inclusion reflect the **prejudice** in a society that makes it hard for some people to succeed. Prejudice and **stereotypes** toward indigenous groups, racial minorities, immigrants, women, or the poor can result in unfair treatment that denies these groups equal opportunities for housing, education, and jobs.

Tolerance for immigrants, religion, and homosexuality

In general, people who come from a foreign country (immigrants) are better tolerated the more similar they are to the majority population of the host country. Immigrants who are of a different race, speak a different language, or practice a different religion can face discrimination that makes it difficult for them to find acceptable housing and jobs. Immigrants in most South American countries experience about the same amount of discrimination as in other countries with similar economies. Uruguay showed relatively more tolerance for immigrants; Bolivia and Guyana showed relatively less.

In nine South American countries more than 50 percent of the people are Roman Catholic. Only in Guyana, Suriname, and Uruguay are Catholics a minority. Eleven South American countries scored high or very high in the category of religious tolerance. Only Colombia scored low and ranked 80th of the 133 SPI countries, in part because a large percentage of Colombians hold anti-Semitic (anti-Jewish) views. Thirty percent of Venezuelans and 24 percent of Argentineans shared these views. Uruguay is one of the countries with very high religious tolerance. It is also one of the least religious countries in South America. Only about 40 percent of Uruguayans say they are affiliated with any particular religion.

Seven South American countries showed a relatively higher level of tolerance for homosexuals than other countries around the world with similar economies. Gay marriage is legal in three countries: Argentina (first in the region to legalize gay marriage, in 2010), Brazil (2013), and Uruguay (2013). The lowest level of tolerance is found in Guyana, and Venezuela showed a relative weakness in this area.

Discrimination and violence against minorities

SPI scores show Colombia, Ecuador, and Peru have the highest rates of discrimination and violence against minorities. South Americans whose ancestors were from Africa (African descent) or were native to the region before the European conquest (indigenous descent) are frequent targets of discrimination The following table shows rankings and the percentages of indigenous and black citizens in each of these countries.

Country	Rank (of 133)	% African Descent	% Indigenous
Colombia	100th	10	3
Ecuador	95th	4	7
Peru	88th	Less than 1	45

Black and Indigenous Minorities in South America

Afro South Americans and indigenous tribes face discrimination in every South American country. Both groups are treated as lower-class citizens and denied opportunities available to other groups.

Afro South Americans descended from the 10 million slaves imported to the continent to work as servants and on plantations and in mines starting in the 1500s. Slavery was outlawed in every South American country by 1888. In 2009 Afro-Peruvian rights organizations presented their own report to the United Nations Committee on the Elimination of Racial Discrimination documenting the ongoing racism, discrimination, and marginalization that their people continue to experience after 400 years on the continent.

South America had thriving civilizations that existed for thousands of years before the European conquest. Millions of the indigenous people died from previously unknown diseases brought unintentionally by the Europeans. Those who didn't die lost their economies and communities. Many were enslaved by the Spanish and Portuguese. Today, dozens of indigenous tribes are spread throughout South America, including the Kayapo and Matipu of Brazil, the Achagua of Colombia and Venezuela, and the Uros of Peru and Bolivia. While indigenous rights are generally protected by law, many native people continue to experience high rates of poverty and face widespread discrimination.

An indigenous child, Mariel, with her two llamas near Lake Titicaca, Bolivia. Bolivia is the poorest country in South America, and almost 70 percent of its population is indigenous.

Access to Advanced Education

Advanced education generally refers to college, or tertiary, education. The average SPI score of 45.35 for South America in the Access to Advanced Education category is just slightly below the world average of 46.24. Based on wealth, scores were lower than expected in Brazil, Chile, Colombia, and Peru in the number of years of education expected compared to the number of years actually completed. The average number of years in school for women in Suriname and Colombia was also relatively low at 8.8 years in both countries. The highest average number of years in school for women was 12.2 in Chile. With an average of 11.1 years, this category was a relative strength for Guyana compared to other countries with similar wealth.

Architecture students work alongside each other in Valparaiso, Chile.

South Americans over age 25 have an average of less than one year of college education. The highest-ranking countries were Colombia with 0.75 year, Chile with 0.53 year, and Brazil with 0.39 year. Not surprisingly, these three countries are among those with the highest number of globally ranked universities on the continent: Brazil with 22, Chile with 11, and Colombia with 9. Argentina has 16 globally ranked universities. Bolivia, Guyana, Paraguay, and Suriname have none. Argentina and Chile have the highest number of students in postsecondary schools, with enrollment rates above 30 percent.

Personal Rights

Having personal rights is a necessary part of having opportunity. Personal rights are protected by law in South America, but the laws are not always enforced. People lose their rights when those who violate them are not held accountable by the police and the courts.

Freedom of movement and association/assembly

People should be able to move around their country and travel to other countries and return. South Americans enjoy unrestricted movement within their own countries and to and from foreign destinations. Colombia scored lower than other South American countries because foreign travel is somewhat restricted.

Freedom to gather peacefully and to associate freely with organizations like political parties and trade unions is a fundamental right listed in the 1948 United Nations' Universal Declaration of Human Rights that every country in South America agreed to. SPI scores show that 5 of the 12 countries enjoy unrestricted freedom of association/assembly. None of the countries suffer extreme restrictions, but 6 of the 12 face some restrictions by the government.

Tens of thousands of university students in Chile have taken to the streets since 2011 to demand a voice in education reforms and to promote free public education for all instead of universities for profit that they say benefit only the rich.

Peaceful protests are legal in every South American country. In Bolivia, Chile, Colombia, Ecuador, Peru, and Venezuela protesters have encountered abusive police or soldiers. Governments are increasingly making serious charges of terrorism against protesters to punish and scare others. Governments are also limiting the activities of NGOs that defend human rights and support protesters. It's not safe in countries like Colombia for people in rural areas to protest because those areas are often controlled by the military or by criminals.

Freedom of speech and political rights

SPI scores in freedom of speech show that the governments in Guyana and Venezuela have complete control of the media, such as newspapers, television, and radio. They tied for a low ranking of 103rd of the 133 SPI countries. Only Chile and Uruguay had no government control; scores in other countries showed some government influence.

For those who enjoy the rights of citizenship and participation in the political process, it can be hard to imagine that some people in the world have no political rights: people who cannot vote or hold public office, have no say in what their government does, and have no right to complain. SPI scores for political rights are shown in the following table.

Score		Country
1	↑ MORE POLITICAL RIGHTS / FEWER POLITICAL RIGHTS ↓	**Chile, Uruguay**
2		**Argentina, Brazil, Guyana, Peru, Suriname**
3		**Bolivia, Colombia, Ecuador, Paraguay**
4		none
5		**Venezuela**
6		none
7		none

Private property rights

Opportunity is limited if individuals, corporations, or the government can take personal property from its rightful owner without fear of being taken to court. The Social Progress Imperative looked at how well the laws protect private property and whether or not those laws are enforced. Scores were measured on a scale of 0 to 100. A score of 0 means that private property is outlawed, all property belongs to the state, and people have no right to sue others and no access to the courts; corruption is everywhere. A score of 100 means that private property is guaranteed by the government, the court system enforces contracts, the justice system punishes those who unlawfully take private property, and there is no corruption or government taking of private property.

Of the 133 countries included in the SPI, 4 South American countries ranked in the bottom 25 percent: Venezuela, Bolivia, Argentina, and Ecuador. Only Chile and Uruguay scored in the top 25 percent.

Text-Dependent Questions

1. Which two minority groups experience the most discrimination in South America?
2. In how many South American countries are more than 70 percent of the people Roman Catholic?
3. The average number of years of school that women finish is highest in which South American country?
4. Which South American country has the lowest GDP per capita?

Research Project

Explore the SPI data online to learn more about the relative social progress of South American countries.

1. Go to the Social Progress Imperative website: socialprogressimperative.org. Click on the Social Progress Index.
2. Click on Display Relative Performance from the list of options on the right of the map. Which South American countries show relative strengths? Weaknesses?
3. With Relative Performance still selected, click on Opportunity. The map changes to show relative strengths and weakness in the Opportunity category. Click back and forth between Social Progress and Opportunity. Notice how relative strengths and weaknesses change depending on which category is selected.
4. Write a page on what you find, especially noting any surprising relationships.

Musicians drumm
at Anata And
harvest festiva
Oruro, Boliv

CHAPTER 4

SOUTH AMERICAN COUNTRIES AT A GLANCE

ARGENTINA 

QUICK STATS

Population: 43,431,886
Urban Population: 91.8 percent of total population
Comparative Size: slightly less than three-tenths the size of the United States
Gross Domestic Product (per capita): $22,600 (78th in the world)
Gross Domestic Product (by sector): agriculture 10.4%, industry 29.5%, services 60.1%
Government: federal republic
Languages: Spanish (official), Italian, English, German, French, indigenous (Mapudungun, Quechua)

A nonpolluting trolley bus provides urban transportation in Cordoba, Argentina.

SOCIAL PROGRESS SNAPSHOT

Social Progress Index: 73.08 (–12.08 below 61.00 world average)
Basic Human Needs: 80.51 (+12.18 above 68.33 world average)
Foundations of Well-being: 73.57 (+7.12 above 66.45 world average)
Opportunity: 65.17 (16.94 above 48.23 world average)

In 1816 the United Provinces of the Rio Plata declared independence from Spain. After Bolivia, Paraguay, and Uruguay formed, the area remaining became Argentina. The country's population and culture were shaped by immigrants from Europe, with the largest percentage from Italy and Spain. Until the mid-20th century, political conflict dominated Argentina's history. After World War II came an era of populism (a movement based on the belief that regular people, not just the wealthy or politically connected, should have control over their government) and military interference in government, including the "Dirty War" of the 1970s, when political dissidents, left-wing rebels, union organizers, students, and others were killed, or "disappeared," by the military and security forces. Estimates of the number of people killed between 1975 and 1978 range from 13,000 to 22,000. Democracy returned in 1983, following a war with Great Britain over the Falkland Islands, and has persisted. Today Argentina has the second-largest economy in South America (Brazil has the largest), although it is dealing with high rates of inflation and unemployment, income inequality, and ongoing financial problems as a result of government debts.

Follow the index every year at socialprogressimperative.org.
Quick Stats from CIA World Factbook.

Bolivia

QUICK STATS

Population: 10,800,882
Urban Population: 68.5 percent of total population
Comparative Size: slightly less than three times the size of Montana
Gross Domestic Product (per capita): $6,200 (158th in the world)
Gross Domestic Product (by sector): agriculture 13.1%, industry 38.9%, services 48%
Government: republic (Note: A new constitution defines Bolivia as a "Social Unitarian State.")
Languages: Spanish (official) 60.7%, Quechua (official) 21.2%, Aymara (official) 14.6%, foreign languages 2.4%, Guarani (official) 0.6%, other native languages 0.4% (official), none 0.1%

SOCIAL PROGRESS SNAPSHOT

Social Progress Index: 63.36 (+2.36 above 61.00 world average)
Basic Human Needs: 67.24 (–1.09 below 68.33 world average)
Foundations of Well-being: 70.86 (+4.41 above 66.45 world average)
Opportunity: 51.98 (+3.75 above 48.23 world average)

Bolivia broke from Spanish rule in 1825. The country was plagued with political instability for many years. Democratic civilian rule was established in 1982. Promising to change the traditional political class and empower the poor, indigenous socialist leader Evo Morales was elected president in 2005 and easily won reelection in 2009 and 2014. In 2016 Morales sought to change the constitution to allow him to run for a fourth term in office, but the change was voted down in a referendum. Corruption scandals and economic problems in the country are threatening the social progress that had been made.

Brazil

QUICK STATS

Population: 204,259,812
Urban Population: 85.7 percent of total population
Comparative Size: slightly smaller than the United States
Gross Domestic Product (per capita): $16,100 (101st in the world)
Gross Domestic Product (by sector): agriculture 5.8%, industry 23.8%, services 70.4%
Government: federal republic
Languages: Portuguese is the official and most widely spoken language; less common languages include Spanish, German, Italian, Japanese, English, and a large number of minor indigenous languages

SOCIAL PROGRESS SNAPSHOT

Social Progress Index: 70.89 (+9.89 above 61.00 world average)
Basic Human Needs: 71.14 (+2.81 above 68.33 world average)
Foundations of Well-being: 76.21 (+9.76 above 66.45 world average)
Opportunity: 65.33 (+17.10 above 48.23 world average)

Following more than three centuries under Portuguese rule, Brazil gained its independence in 1822, maintaining a monarchical system of government until the abolition of slavery in 1888 and the subsequent proclamation of a republic. Brazilian coffee exporters politically dominated the country until 1930. Brazil underwent more than a half century of populist and military government until 1985, when the military regime peacefully ceded power to civilian rulers.

A grandfather and granddaughter share a book together in Valparaiso, Chile.

CHILE 

QUICK STATS

Population: 17,508,260
Urban Population: 89.5 percent of total population
Comparative Size: slightly smaller than twice the size of Montana
Gross Domestic Product (per capita): $23,000 (76th in the world)
Gross Domestic Product (by sector): agriculture 3.5%, industry 35.5%, services 61.1%
Government: republic
Languages: Spanish 99.5% (official), English 10.2%, indigenous 1% (includes Mapudungun, Aymara, Quechua, Rapa Nui), other 2.3%, unspecified 0.2%

SOCIAL PROGRESS SNAPSHOT

Social Progress Index: 78.29 (+17.29 above 61.00 world average)
Basic Human Needs: 86.32 (+17.99 above 68.33 world average)
Foundations of Well-being: 74.85 (+8.40 above 66.45 world average)
Opportunity: 73.69 (+25.46 above 48.23 world average)

Before the Spanish arrived in the 16th century, Chile was inhabited by the Inca and the Mapuche. Chile won independence from Spain in 1818. It defeated Peru and Bolivia to win its northern regions. An elected Marxist government was overthrown in 1973 by a military coup. A freely elected president was inaugurated in 1990. Chile has increasingly assumed regional and international leadership roles befitting its status as a stable, democratic nation.

COLOMBIA 

QUICK STATS

Population: 46,736,728
Urban Population: 76.4 percent of total population
Comparative Size: slightly less than twice the size of Texas
Gross Domestic Product (per capita): $13,400 (111th in the world)
Gross Domestic Product (by sector): agriculture, 6.1%, industry 37.3%, services 56.6%
Government: republic; executive branch dominates government structure
Language: Spanish (official)

Life is happening in downtown Bogotá, Colombia.

SOCIAL PROGRESS SNAPSHOT

Social Progress Index: 68.85 (+7.85 above 61.00 world average)
Basic Human Needs: 70.98 (+2.65 above 68.33 world average)
Foundations of Well-being: 77.30 (+10.85 above 66.45 world average)
Opportunity: 58.26 (+10.03 above 48.23 world average)

Colombia was one of three countries that emerged from the collapse of Gran Colombia in 1830. An almost 50-year conflict between government forces and antigovernment groups, principally funded by the drug trade, escalated during the 1990s. In 2012 the Colombian government started peace negotiations and increased efforts to reassert control throughout the country. Despite decades of conflict and drug-related security challenges, Colombia maintains relatively strong democratic institutions, transparent elections, and the protection of civil liberties.

ECUADOR 

Children play with puzzle pieces at the Natural Sciences Museum in Quito, Ecuador, as part of an initiative to tighten the ties between museums and the local community.

QUICK STATS

Population: 15,868,396
Urban Population: 63.7 percent of total population
Comparative Size: slightly smaller than Nevada
Gross Domestic Product (per capita): $11,200 (123rd in the world)
Gross Domestic Product (by sector): agriculture 6%, industry 34.4%, services 59.6%
Government: republic
Languages: Spanish (Castilian) 93% (official), Quechua 4.1%, other indigenous 0.7%, foreign 2.2%

SOCIAL PROGRESS SNAPSHOT

Social Progress Index: 68.25 (+7.25 above 61.00 world average)
Basic Human Needs: 73.56 (+5.23 above 68.33 world average)
Foundations of Well-being: 76.46 (+10.01 above 66.45 world average)
Opportunity: 54.72 (+6.49 above 48.23 world average)

Ecuador was part of the Inca Empire until the Spanish conquest. Quito became a seat of colonial government in 1563 and part of the Viceroyalty of New Granada in 1717. The territories of the Viceroyalty (Colombia, Venezuela, and Quito) gained independence (1819–1822) and formed Gran Colombia. Quito withdrew in 1830 and changed the name to Republic of the Equator. Civil government came to Ecuador in 1974. In 2008 voters approved the 20th constitution since independence.

GUYANA 

QUICK STATS

Population: 735,222
Urban Population: 28.6 percent of total population
Comparative Size: slightly smaller than Idaho
Gross Domestic Product (per capita): $6,900 (154th in the world)
Gross Domestic Product (by sector): agriculture 20.3%, industry 39.2%, services 40.5%
Government: republic
Languages: English (official), Guyanese Creole, indigenous languages (including Caribbean and Arawak languages), Indian languages (including Caribbean Hindustani, a dialect of Hindi), Chinese

SOCIAL PROGRESS SNAPSHOT

Social Progress Index: 60.42 (–0.58 below 61.00 world average)
Basic Human Needs: 68.80 (+.47 above 68.33 world average)
Foundations of Well-being: 60.57 (–5.88 below 66.45 world average)
Opportunity: 51.89 (+3.66 above 48.23 world average)

Originally a Dutch colony in the 17th century, by 1815 Guyana had become a British possession. The abolition of slavery led to settlement of urban areas by former slaves and the importation of servants from India to work the sugar plantations. The resulting divide has persisted and has led to turbulent politics. Guyana achieved independence from the UK in 1966, and since then it has been ruled mostly by socialist-oriented governments.

PARAGUAY 

Residents use boats to cross a flooded street in Paraguay.

QUICK STATS

Population: 6,783,272
Urban Population: 59.7 percent of total population
Comparative Size: slightly smaller than California
Gross Domestic Product (per capita): $8,400 (138th in the world)
Gross Domestic Product (by sector): agriculture 19.9%, industry 17.6%, services 62.5%
Government: constitutional republic
Languages: Spanish (official), Guarani (official)

SOCIAL PROGRESS SNAPSHOT

Social Progress Index: 67.10 (+6.10 above 61.00 world average)
Basic Human Needs: 71.11 (+2.78 above 68.33 world average)
Foundations of Well-being: 71.11 (+4.66 above 66.45 world average)
Opportunity: 59.09 (+10.86 above 48.23 world average)

Paraguay achieved independence from Spain in 1811. In the War of the Triple Alliance (1865–1870) between Paraguay and Argentina, Brazil, and Uruguay, Paraguay lost two-thirds of its adult males and much territory. Its economy stagnated for the next half century. Following the Chaco War of 1932–1835 with Bolivia, Paraguay gained a large part of the Chaco lowlands. Paraguay has had relatively free and regular elections since its return to democracy in 1989.

PERU 

QUICK STATS

Population: 30,444,999
Urban Population: 78.6 percent of total population
Comparative Size: almost twice the size of Texas; slightly smaller than Alaska
Gross Domestic Product (per capita): $11,800 (119th in the world)
Gross Domestic Product (by sector): agriculture 7.1%, industry 36.7%, services 56.2%
Government: constitutional republic
Languages: Spanish (official) 84.1%, Quechua (official) 13%, Aymara (official) 1.7%, Ashaninka 0.3%, other native languages 0.7%, other 0.2%

SOCIAL PROGRESS SNAPSHOT

Social Progress Index: 67.23 (+6.23 above 61.00 world average)
Basic Human Needs: 69.89 (+1.56 above 68.33 world average)
Foundations of Well-being: 73.89 (+7.44 above 66.45 world average)
Opportunity: 57.92 (+9.69 above 48.23 world average)

Ancient Peru was the seat of several prominent Andean civilizations, most notably that of the Incas, whose empire was captured by the Spanish in 1533. Peruvian independence was declared in 1821, and the Spanish forces were defeated in 1824. After a dozen years of military rule, Peru returned to democratic leadership in 1980. Peru's first president of indigenous ethnicity, Alejandro Toledo Manrique, was democratically elected in 2001.

Suriname 

QUICK STATS

Population: 579,633
Urban Population: 66 percent of total population
Comparative Size: slightly larger than Georgia
Gross Domestic Product (per capita): $16,600 (94th in the world)
Gross Domestic Product (by sector): agriculture 8.6%, industry 37.3%, services 54.1%
Government: constitutional democracy
Languages: Dutch (official), English (widely spoken), Sranang Tongo (native language of Creoles and much of the younger population), Caribbean Hindustani (a dialect of Hindi), Javanese

SOCIAL PROGRESS SNAPSHOT

Foundations of Well-being: 75.40 (+8.95 above 66.45 world average)
Opportunity: 58.02 (+9.79 above 48.23 world average)

First explored by the Spaniards in the 16th century and then settled by the English in the mid-17th century, Suriname became a Dutch colony in 1667. With the abolition of African slavery in 1863, workers were brought from India and Java. The Netherlands granted the colony independence in 1975. International pressure forced Suriname's first democratic election, which was held in 1987.

Uruguay 

QUICK STATS

Population: 3,341,893
Urban Population: 95.3 percent of total population
Comparative Size: slightly smaller than the state of Washington
Gross Domestic Product (per capita): $20,600 (80th in the world)
Gross Domestic Product (by sector): agriculture 7.5%, industry 20.4%, services 72.1%
Government: constitutional republic
Languages: Spanish (official), Portunol, Brazilero (Portuguese-Spanish mix on the Brazilian frontier)

A wind park of 25 2-megawatt wind turbines operates in Maldonado, Uruguay.

SOCIAL PROGRESS SNAPSHOT

Social Progress Index: 79.21 (+18.21 above 61.00 world average)
Basic Human Needs: 86.18 (+17.85 above 68.33 world average)
Foundations of Well-being: 75.03 (+8.58 above 66.45 world average)
Opportunity: 76.41 (+28.18 above 48.23 world average)

Montevideo, founded in 1726 as a Spanish stronghold and the capital of Uruguay today, used its harbor to become a commercial center. Claimed by Argentina but annexed by Brazil in 1821, Uruguay secured freedom in 1828. A Marxist movement launched in the 1960s led Uruguay's president to give control to the military in 1973. Civilian rule was not restored until 1985. In 2004 a left-of-center coalition won national elections. Uruguay's political and labor conditions are among the freest on the continent.

Supporters of Sucre Mayor Carlos Ocariz greet him at the National Assembly in Caracas, Venezuela, where the mayors of other localities of Caracas along with opposition deputies presented a project to decentralize public services and the creation of a special police body for the city.

VENEZUELA

QUICK STATS

Population: 29,275,460
Urban Population: 89 percent of total population
Comparative Size: almost six times the size of Georgia; slightly more than twice the size of California
Gross Domestic Product (per capita): $17,700 (88th in the world)
Gross Domestic Product (by sector): agriculture 3.8%, industry 35.4%, services 60.8%
Government: federal republic
Languages: Spanish (official), numerous indigenous dialects

SOCIAL PROGRESS SNAPSHOT

Social Progress Index: 63.45 (+2.45 above 61.00 world average)
Basic Human Needs: 66.12 (–2.21 below 68.33 world average)
Foundations of Well-being: 74.69 (+8.24 above 66.45 world average)
Opportunity: 49.55 (+1.32 above 48.23 world average)

Venezuela was one of three countries that emerged from Gran Colombia in 1830. For most of the first half of the 20th century, Venezuela was ruled by military dictators who promoted the oil industry and allowed some social reforms. Democratic elections have been held since 1959. Under President Hugo Chávez (1999–2013) and his successor, Nicolás Maduro, the government has become increasingly authoritarian, democratic institutions have deteriorated, and threats to freedom of expression have increased.

Conclusion

If South America were a country, a Social Progress Snapshot like those in Chapter 4 could be calculated by averaging the scores of the 11 ranked SPI countries. Using simple averages, South America's ratings might look like this:

SOCIAL PROGRESS SNAPSHOT FOR SOUTH AMERICA

Social Progress Index: 69.10 (+4.71 above 64.39 world average)
Basic Human Needs: 73.35 (+5.65 above 70.82 world average)
Foundations of Well-being: 73.68 (+6.00 above 67.68 world average)
Opportunity: 60.17 (+8.14 above 52.03 world average)

In this volume, we've seen that wealthier countries often have higher social progress scores. The two countries with the highest GDP per capita, Uruguay and Chile, also had the highest social progress scores. Their scores were also high compared to other countries around the world with similar economies. Bolivia and Guyana, the two poorest countries, had the lowest scores; both showed relative strengths in some categories compared to other poor countries. Even so, income did not always equal more social progress. Venezuela, with a GDP per capita similar to that of Uruguay's, scored only slightly higher in social progress than Bolivia.

We've also seen that a high score does not always mean social progress for everyone. Racial and ethnic minorities, immigrants, and rural populations often don't have the same access to food, housing, medical care, and education that other groups enjoy. Poverty and discrimination deny people their basic rights and limit their access to the courts.

Ranking the scores revealed relative strengths and weaknesses in each country based on the size of its economy. Examining relative weaknesses is important because they show countries where others with similar resources are doing a better job, which may give them ideas or the motivation to make changes. For example, Argentina has room for improvement in providing shelter, protecting personal safety, and defending personal rights. Bolivia needs better sanitation and more affordable housing. Guyana needs to increase enrollment in primary school and improve access to health care. Most countries need to make improvements in ecosystem sustainability.

In the past, economic growth was used as the only measure of success. Today, the work of the Social Progress Imperative is helping us to understand that real success must consider social progress and that social progress must benefit everyone.

A worker walks the subterranean level of the Itaipu hydroelectric power station, shared between Brazil and Paraguay.

Revelers from the Alegria da Zona Sul samba school participate in the annual Carnival parade at the Sambadrome in Rio de Janeiro, Brazil.

Series Glossary

Anemia: a condition in which the blood doesn't have enough healthy red blood cells, most often caused by not having enough iron

Aquifer: an underground layer of water-bearing permeable rock, from which groundwater can be extracted using a water well

Asylum: protection granted by a nation to someone who has left their native country as a political refugee

Basic human needs: the things people need to stay alive: clean water, sanitation, food, shelter, basic medical care, safety

Biodiversity: the variety of life that is absolutely essential to the health of different ecosystems

Carbon dioxide (CO_2): a greenhouse gas that contributes to global warming and climate change

Censorship: the practice of officially examining books, movies, and other media and art, and suppressing unacceptable parts

Child mortality rate: the number of children that die before their fifth birthday for every 1,000 babies born alive

Communicable diseases: medical conditions spread by airborne viruses or bacteria or through bodily fluids such as malaria, tuberculosis, and HIV/AIDS; also called **infectious diseases;** differ from **noncommunicable diseases**, medical conditions not caused by infection and requiring long-term treatment such as diabetes or heart disease

Contraception: any form of birth control used to prevent pregnancy

Corruption: the dishonest behavior by people in positions of power for their own benefit

Deforestation: the clearing of trees, transforming a forest into cleared land

Desalination: a process that removes minerals (including salt) from ocean water

Discrimination: the unjust or prejudicial treatment of different categories of people, especially on the grounds of race, age, or sex

Ecosystem: a biological community of interacting organisms and their physical environment

Ecosystem sustainability: when we care for resources like clean air, water, plants, and animals so that they will be available to future generations

Emissions: the production and discharge of something, especially gas or radiation

Ethnicities: social groups that have a common national or cultural tradition

Extremism: the holding of extreme political or religious views; fanaticism

Famine: a widespread scarcity of food that results in malnutrition and starvation on a large scale

Food desert: a neighborhood or community with no walking access to affordable, nutritious food

Food security: having enough to eat at all times

Greenhouse gas emissions: any of the atmospheric gases that contribute to the greenhouse effect by absorbing infrared radiation produced by solar warming of the earth's surface. They include carbon dioxide (CO_2), methane (CH_4), nitrous oxide (NO_2), and water vapor.

Gross domestic product (GDP): the total value of all products and services created in a country during a year

GDP per capita (per person): the gross domestic product divided by the number of people in the country. For example, if the GDP for a country is one hundred million dollars ($100,000,000) and the population is one million people (1,000,000), then the GDP per capita (value created per person) is $100.

Habitat: environment for a plant or animal, including climate, food, water, and shelter

Incarceration: the condition of being imprisoned

Income inequality: when the wealth of a country is spread very unevenly among the population

Indigenous people: culturally distinct groups with long-standing ties to the land in a specific area

Inflation: when the same amount money buys less from one day to the next. Just because things cost more does not mean that people have more money. Low-income people trapped in a high inflation economy can quickly find themselves unable to purchase even the basics like food.

Infrastructure: permanent features required for an economy to operate such as transportation routes and electric grids; also systems such as education and courts

Latrine: a communal outdoor toilet, such as a trench dug in the ground

Literate: able to read and write

Malnutrition: lack of proper nutrition, caused by not having enough to eat, not eating enough of the right things, or being unable to use the food that one does eat

Maternal mortality rate: the number of pregnant women who die for every 100,000 births.

Natural resources: industrial materials and assets provided by nature such as metal deposits, timber, and water

Nongovernmental organization (NGO): a nonprofit, voluntary citizens' group organized on a local, national, or international level. Examples include organizations that support human rights, advocate for political participation, and work for improved health care.

Parliament: a group of people who are responsible for making the laws in some kinds of government

Prejudice: an opinion that isn't based on facts or reason

Preventive care: health care that helps an individual avoid illness

Primary school: includes grades 1–6 (also known as elementary school); precedes **secondary** and **tertiary education**, schooling beyond the primary grades; secondary generally corresponds to high school, and tertiary generally means college-level

Privatization: the transfer of ownership, property, or business from the government to the private sector (the part of the national economy that is not under direct government control)

Sanitation: conditions relating to public health, especially the provision of clean drinking water and adequate sewage disposal

Stereotypes: are common beliefs about the nature of the members of a specific group that are based on limited experience or incorrect information

Subsistence agriculture: a system of farming that supplies the needs of the farm family without generating any surplus for sale

Surface water: the water found above ground in streams, lakes, and rivers

Tolerance: a fair, objective, and permissive attitude toward those whose opinions, beliefs, practices, racial or ethnic origins, and so on differ from one's own

Trafficking: dealing or trading in something illegal

Transparency: means that the government operates in a way that is visible to and understood by the public

Universal health care: a system in which every person in a country has access to doctors and hospitals

Urbanization: the process by which towns and cities are formed and become larger as more and more people begin living and working in central areas

Well-being: the feeling people have when they are healthy, comfortable, and happy

Whistleblower: someone who reveals private information about the illegal activities of a person or organization

Index

RESOURCES

Continue exploring the world of development through this assortment of online and print resources. Follow links, stay organized, and maintain a critical perspective. Also, seek out news sources from outside the country in which you live.

Websites

Social Progress Imperative: socialprogressimperative.org

United Nations—Human Development Indicators: hdr.undp.org/en/countries and Sustainable Development Goals: un.org/sustainabledevelopment/sustainable-development-goals

World Bank—World Development Indicators: data.worldbank.org/data-catalog/world-development-indicators

World Health Organization—country statistics: who.int/gho/countries/en

U.S. State Department—human rights tracking site: humanrights.gov/dyn/countries.html

Oxfam International: oxfam.org/en

Amnesty International: amnesty.org/en

Human Rights Watch: hrw.org

Reporters without Borders: en.rsf.org

CIA—The World Factbook: cia.gov/library/publications/the-world-factbook

Books

Literary and classics

The Good Earth, Pearl S. Buck

Grapes of Wrath, John Steinbeck

The Jungle, Upton Sinclair

Nonfiction—historical/classic

Angela's Ashes, Frank McCourt

Lakota Woman, Mary Crow Dog with Richard Erdoes

Orientalism, Edward Said

Silent Spring, Rachel Carson

The Souls of Black Folk, W.E.B. Du Bois

Nonfiction: development and policy—presenting a range of views

Behind the Beautiful Forevers: Life, Death, and Hope in a Mumbai Undercity, Katherine Boo

The Bottom Billion: Why the Poorest Countries Are Failing and What Can Be Done About It, Paul Collier

The End of Poverty, Jeffrey D. Sachs

For the Common Good: Redirecting the Economy toward Community, the Environment, and a Sustainable Future, Herman E. Daly

I Am Malala: The Girl Who Stood Up for Education and Was Shot by the Taliban, Malala Yousafzai and Christina Lamb

The Life You Can Save: Acting Now to End World Poverty, Peter Singer

Mismeasuring Our Lives: Why GDP Doesn't Add Up, Joseph E. Stiglitz, Amartya Sen, and Jean-Paul Fitoussi

Rachel and Her Children: Homeless Families in America, Jonathan Kozol

The White Man's Burden: Why the West's Efforts to Aid the Rest Have Done So Much Ill and So Little Good, William Easterly

Foreword writer Michael Green is an economist, author, and cofounder of the Social Progressive Imperative. A UK native and graduate of Oxford University, Green has worked in aid and development for the British government and taught economics at Warsaw University.

Author Judy Boyd has designed and developed self-study workbooks, instructor-led courses, and online learning modules to teach language, technology, and mapping. She holds a B.S. in cartography and an M.S. in interactive telecommunications. She lives in Santa Fe, New Mexico, where she works as a freelance writer and watercolor artist.

Picture credits: 10, ekler/Shutterstock; 13, Carlos Garcia Granthon/ZUMA Press/Newscom; 14, Andres Cristaldo/EPA/Newscom, 18, photosvit/iStock; 20, Martin Alipaz./EPA/Newscom; 22, SuSanA Secretariat (CC by 2.0 https://commons.wikimedia.org/wiki/File:Waiting_eagerly_for_the_water_tank_(3109524599).jpg#/media/File:Waiting_eagerly_for_the_water_tank_(3109524599).jpg); 23, Mike and Amanda Knowles (CC by-SA 2.0 https://commons.wikimedia.org/wiki/File:Cuy_in_the_kitchen.jpg]; 24, Ketzirah Lesser and Art Drauglis (CC by SA-2.0 https://www.flickr.com/photos/wiredwitch/11330939353); 30, Haroldo Palo Jr/KINO/VWPICS/Newscom; 34, David Snyder/ZUMAPRESS/Newscom; 37, BPC Sala de Internet by Wbohorquezm—Own work. (CC by-SA 3.0, https://commons.wikimedia.org/w/index.php?curid=9509659; 40, CHINE NOUVELLE/SIPA/Newscom; 42, taboga/Shutterstock; Ondrej Prosicky/Shutterstock], 45; Expedition 29 Crew, courtesy of NASA. Derivative work, Julian Herzog (ISS029-E-8032) [https://upload.wikimedia.org/wikipedia/commons/1/1c/ISS029-E-008032_Fires_along_the_Rio_Xingu_-_Brazil.jpg; 48, Jose Je/EPA/Newscom; 51, Sergio Goya/picture-alliance/dpa/Newscom; 52, https://commons.wikimedia.org/wiki/File%3AIndifference.jpg; 54, Jamez42 (Own work) [CC0]]; 57, Ben Pipe/robertharding/Newscom; 58, Design Pics/Peter Langer/Newscom; 60, erlucho/iStock; 64, Christian Kober/robertharding/Newscom; 65, Holger Mette/iStock; 67, REB Images Blend Images/Newscom; 67, mtcurado/iStock; 68, José Jácome/EFE/Newscom; 69, Andres Cristaldo/EPA/Newscom; 70, Iván Franco/EFE/Newscom; 71, Miguel Gutiérrez/EFE/Newscom, 73, Santi Carneri/EFE/Newscom; 74, Chine Nouvelle/SIPA/Newscom
Front cover: clockwise, from upper left: Bill Bachmann/Photoshot/Newscom (Argentina); marchello74/iStock (Brazil); Ruslana Iurchenko/Shutterstock (Peru); Chine Nouvelle/SIPA/Newscom (Uruguay)